To Nan.
from Diane.
Christmas 1992

COUNTRY
TREASURY

—————————— *The* ——————————
$\mathcal{C}$ountry $\mathcal{T}$reasury
Collection

Spring
The Hedgerow
The Meadow
The Watermill
The Farmyard
The Clifftop
The Country Estate

Summer
The Village Green
The River Bank
The Cottage Garden
The Green Lane
The Herb Garden
The Seashore

Autumn
The Orchard
The Farmland
The Wood
The Downs
The Harbour
The Moors

Winter
The Churchyard
The Country Park
The Mountains
The Forest Glade
The Sporting Covert
The Canal

*Where possible, brief biographical notes on the writers featured
are included at the end of each volume.*

Front cover: *Badgers by J. G. Millais*
Details of the paintings and other illustrations in this book are given on the last page.

This compilation is the copyright © 1991 of Marshall Cavendish Limited.

Published in 1991 for THE COUNTRY TREASURY by Marshall Cavendish Partworks Ltd;
119, Wardour Street, London W1V 3TD. Printed and bound in Spain by
Printer Industria Grafica, Barcelona.

ISBN 0-7485-3473-3

Autumn

The Downs

*T*he Downs have always held a special magic for ramblers and botanists. The gentle crescent of chalk uplands, curving down from the Northeast to the western tip of Dorset in the South, is lonely and wild yet infinitely rich in rare plants and insects.

The juniper thrives in this landscape, and the surface of the Downs is carpeted with acres of wild thyme, purple and fragrant right into Autumn, ravishing the senses with its beauty.

Underground, badgers tunnel deep into the earth to make their homes. These shy creatures emerge only at night, sniffing cautiously. Their nocturnal search for food is accompanied by much snuffling and grunting.

Meanwhile, soaring majestically above it all is the glorious kestrel, hovering in the wind, keen-eyed for prey, prince of the air.

Wild Thyme

*I*t was a great favourite of Francis Bacon, who, in giving us his plan for the perfect garden, directs that alleys should be planted with fragrant flowers: 'burnet, wild thyme and watermints, which perfume the air most delightfully being trodden upon and crushed,' so that you may 'have pleasure where you walk or tread'. The herb, wherever it grows wild, denotes a pure atmosphere, and was thought to enliven the spirits by the fragrance which it diffuses into the air around it.

In its most natural state, when found on dry exposed downs, it is small and procumbent, often forming dense cushions.

M. Grieve:
MODERN HERBAL

'I Know a Bank'

William Shakespeare 1564-1616

'I know a bank whereon the wild thyme blows,
Where ox-lips and the nodding violet grows;
Quite over-canopied with lush woodbine,
With sweet musk roses, and with eglantine:
There sleeps Titania sometime of the night,
Lulled in these flowers with dances and delight;
And there the snake throws her enamell'd skin,
Weed wide enough to wrap a fairy in...'

A Bed of Thyme

W. H. Hudson 1841-1922

Among the bushes on the lower slopes one stumbles on places of extraordinary fertility, where the thistle, foxglove, ragwort, viper's bugloss, agrimony and wild mignonette grow to a man's breast; while over them all the mullein lifts its greatest flowery rod to a height of six to nine feet. From these luxuriant patches you pass to more open ground covered with golden seeding grasses, and heather, fiery, purple-red, and emerald-green spots powdered white with woodruff, and great beds of purple thyme. One afternoon, tired with a long day's ramble in the burning sun, I cast myself down on one of these fragrant beds and almost fell asleep. That night when I threw off my clothes I noticed that the fragrance still clung to them, and when I woke next morning the air of the room was so charged with it that for a moment I fancied myself still out of doors resting on that purple flowery bed.

How to See the Fairies

Anon c. 16th century

To enable one to see the fairies. A pint of sallet oyle and put it into a vial glasse: and first wash it with rose-water and marigolde water: the flowers to be gathered towards the east. Wash it till the oyle becomes white, then put it into the glasse, and then put thereto the budds of hollyhocke, the flowers of marygolde, the flowers or toppes of wilde thyme, the budds of young hazel, and the thyme must be gathered near the side of a hill where fairies used to be; and take the grasse of a fairy throne, then all these put into the oyle in the glasse and settle it to dissolve three dayes in the sun, and then keep it for thy use.

BRAVE THYME

Thyme is a symbol of courage in the language of flowers. In Lancastrian days, ladies embroidered a motif of a bee hovering over thyme on scarves which they gave to their knights.

THYME FOR BEES

The wonderful scent of wild thyme is irresistible to bees, and the honey they make from it is particularly delicious.

FLOWERS OF THYME

Wild thyme has beautiful purple flowers, which cover the Downs in a fragrant carpet.

SWEET DREAMS!

The Scots believed that drinking tea made from wild thyme prevented nightmares.

SCENTED SHEEP

Shepherds on the Downs believe that Downland sheep have a fine flavour from grazing on the thyme.

THE FAIRY HERB

Wild thyme has always been associated with the fairies — hence the fairy queen Titania and her attendants could be found 'on a bank whereon the wild thyme blows' in Shakespeare's A MIDSUMMER NIGHT'S DREAM.

BATHTIME

Wild thyme was used in hot baths to relax muscles, to cure rheumatism, and to heal wounds.

TOOTHSOME THYME

Thyme has always been a favourite herb for use as an antiseptic mouthwash, a gargle, and in toothpaste.

The Juniper

The juniper is the gin-tree, its pungent berries flavouring gin, to which service the tree owes its name, from the French for gin, genièvre. Berries and foliage alike give forth a pleasant resinous fragrance. The many forms that the shrub will take is made evident on the North Downs of Surrey, especially on the hill called Juniper, near Mickleham. The stalwart little tree is also smothering parts of the Chilterns not yet invaded by the beech.

Marcus Woodward:
THE NEW BOOK OF TREES

Junipers on the Downs

Anthony Collett c. 1907

Most typical of all the downland bushes is the dark, evergreen juniper, that still flecks many of the steeper slopes of thyme-scented sward with its dappled, primaeval growth as thickly as the clouds in a mackerel sky, or the white forms of the pasturing sheep that roam among its own darker archipelagoes. On the more exposed hillsides the juniper-bushes are wind-clipped, round, and stunted in their growth; but within the sheltering curves of the smooth, unbroken hills, or where they yield one another mutual support in a denser thicket beside some wind-breaking thorn, they shoot forth in loose, feathery sprays of an inimitably graceful wildness. In early summer the young shoots of the year are frosted with a silvery bloom that brightens their dark evergreen boughs with an austere and tender freshness, a beauty wholly in accord with the restrained simplicity of the unbroken curves of the great chalk downs; and this same puritan contrast of dark and silvery hues is presented by most other of the dominant tree-growths of the chalk.

The Combe

Edward Thomas 1878-1917

The Combe was ever dark, ancient and dark.
Its mouth is stopped with bramble, thorn, and briar;
And no one scrambles over the sliding chalk
By beech and yew and perishing juniper
Down the half precipices of its sides, with roots
And rabbit holes for steps. The sun of Winter,
And moon of Summer, and all the singing birds
Except the missel-thrush that loves juniper,
Are quite shut out. But far more ancient and dark
The Combe looks since they killed the badger there,
Dug him out and gave him to the hounds,
That most ancient Briton of English beasts.

SILVER AND GREEN

The sharp, awl-shaped leaves grow in whorls of three, and are green on one side, silver on the other. They are evergreen.

PENCIL LINES

Pencils that are said to be made from cedar wood are more likely to be made from juniper.

TOPIARY SHAPES

FRUIT FOR THE BIRDS

When fully grown the blue-black juniper berries are the size of a pea, and are dispersed by birds.

Long ago, the juniper was popular for topiary work, and was trained into the shapes of open bowls or goblets.

Juniper Berries

DIVINE PROTECTION

According to legend, the juniper was the tree that sheltered the infant Jesus on the flight into Egypt.

A TASTE OF GIN

The fresh, distinctive taste of gin is derived from juniper berries which are used for the flavouring.

FUNERAL PYRES

The ancients consecrated juniper to the Furies, and threw its berries on funeral pyres to protect the departing spirit from evil.

The Kestrel

*T*he Kestrel, the commonest hawk in most parts of Britain, is both resident and migratory.

In addition to its chestnut dress and broadly barred tail, the flight of the "Wind-hover" is a sure sign of its identity, for though other hawks hover none has so perfected the art. It hangs twenty to thirty feet above the earth, poised in the air with quivering wings and wide-spread, depressed tail, then slides forward, often without a wing-beat, to halt once more over a fresh patch of ground. For a second or two the swiftly winnowing wings may be held motionless, the bird supported by an air current. Having sighted quarry when hovering, it dives headlong with almost closed wings, checks itself close to the ground, seizes its victim and mounts again.

T.A. Coward:
BIRDS OF THE WAYSIDE AND WOODLAND

Up on the Downs

John Masefield 1878-1967

Up on the downs the red-eyed kestrels hover,
Eyeing the grass.
The field-mouse flits like a shadow into cover
As their shadows pass.

Men are burning the gorse on the down's shoulder;
A drift of smoke
Glitters with fire and hangs, and the skies smoulder,
And the lungs choke.

Once the tribe did thus on the downs, on these downs
burning
Men in the frame,
Crying to the gods of the downs till their brains were
turning
And the gods came.

And to-day on the downs, in the wind, the hawks, the
grasses,
In blood and air,
Something passes me and cries as it passes,
On the chalk downland bare.

Taming
the
Kestrel

W. H. Hudson 1841-1922

The kestrel is easier to tame, and, when tame, more docile and affectionate, than most hawks, and many accounts have appeared in print of the bird and its ways in the domestic condition; but, to my mind, not one so interesting as the history of a pet kestrel kept a few years since by some friends of mine. The bird was young when it came into their hands, and was lovingly cared for, and made free of a large house and park, and of the whole wide country beyond. And it made good use of its liberty. As a rule, every morning it would fly away and disappear from sight until the evening, when, some time before sunset, it would return, dash in at the open door, and perch on some

elevated situation – a cornice, or bust, or on the top of a
large picture-frame. Invariably at dinner time it flew to
the dining room, and would then settle on the shoulder
of its master or mistress, to be fed with small scraps of
meat. This pleasant state of things lasted for about three

years, during which time the bird always roosted in, or somewhere near, the house, flew abroad by day, to return faithfully every evening to his loving human friends to be caressed, and fed, and made much of; and it might have continued several years longer, down to the present time, if the bird's temper had not suffered a mysterious change. All at once, for no reason that anyone could guess, he became subject to the most extraordinary outbreaks of ill-temper, and in such a state he would, on his return from his daily wanderings abroad, violently attack some person in the room. Up till this time he had preferred his master and mistress to any other member of the household, and had shown an equal attachment to both; now he would single out one or other of these his best friends for his most violent attacks; and, very curiously, on the day when he attacked his master he would display the usual affection towards his mistress, but on the next day would reverse the process. And his hostility was not to be despised: rising up into the air to a good height, he would dash down with great force on to the obnoxious person's head, often inflicting a lacerating blow with his claws. More than once, the lady told me, after one of these cutting, ungrateful blows on her forehead her face was bathed in blood.

It is pleasant to be able to relate that no feeling of resentment or alarm was excited by this behaviour on the part of the bird; that he was never deprived of his sweet liberty or treated with less gentleness than before. It was hoped and believed that he would outgrow the savage fit, and if he had confined his virulent attacks to his master and mistress it would have been well with him. Unfortunately for him, he attacked others who were made of poorer clay. One evening at dinner the butler, while occupied with his duties, was struck savagely on the

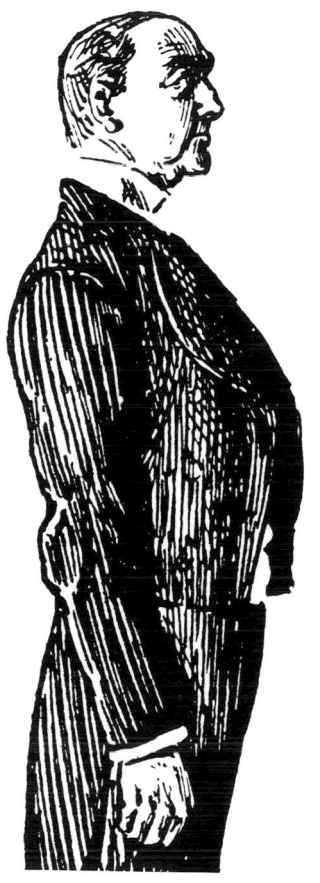

wrist by the kestrel. Like a well-trained servant, he did not wince or cry out, but marched stolidly round the table, pouring out wine, anxious only to conceal the blood that trickled from his wounds. But on the following day the bird was missing, and was never afterwards seen or heard of.

The Windhover

Gerard Manley Hopkins 1844-1889

I caught this morning morning's minion kingdom of
daylight's dauphin, dapple-dawn-drawn falcon, in his
riding
Of the rolling level underneath him steady air, and
striding
High there, how he rung upon the rein of a wimpling
wing
In his ecstasy! then off, off forth on swing,
As a skate's heel sweeps smooth on a bow-bend: the hurl
and gliding
Rebuffed the big wind. My heart in hiding
Stirred for a bird, – the achieve of, the mastery of the
thing!

Brute beauty and valour and act, oh, air, pride, plume,
here
Buckle! And the fire that breaks from thee then, a billion
Times told lovelier, more dangerous, O my Chevalier!

No wonder of it: shéer plód makes plough down sillion
Shine, and blue-bleak embers, ah my dear,
Fall, gall themselves, and gash gold-vermilion.

HOVERING FLIGHT

The flight of the kestrel is unique. It has a distinctive way of hovering over its prey, hanging motionless in the air, apart from its beating wings.

THE MINIMALIST NEST

The kestrel does not make much of a nest — it lays four to five eggs on a rock ledge, in a scratched-out hollow, a church-tower, ruin or quarry, or a deserted nest.

CALL NOTES

The call is a clear and distinctive 'kee, kee'.

LARK FEAST

The Latin name for the kestrel (alaudarius) means 'an eater of larks'. In fact, mice and field voles are its favourite prey, and it will also eat frogs, small birds and beetles.

TAME KESTRELS

Historically, kestrels have often been tamed and used for hunting. Chicks were removed from the nest, and hand-reared, before being introduced to the hoods and jesses (right) used to carry the bird quietly.

KESTREL EGGS

The kestrel lays four or five eggs in April or May. They are blotched with dull red on a reddish ground.

SPORTING FEATHERS

Huntsmen used to try and procure the wing feather of a kestrel to wear in their caps, since they believed it would help them to get good sport.

The Badger

The badger's legs are so short, that its belly seems to touch the ground; this however is but a deceitful appearance, as it is caused by the length of the hair, which is very long all over the body, and makes it seem much more bulky than it really is. It is a solitary slow-moving animal, that finds refuge, remote from man, and digs itself a deep hole, with great assiduity. It seems to avoid the light, and seldom quits its retreat by day, only stealing out at night to find subsistence. It burrows in the ground very easily, its legs being short and strong, and its claws, stiff and horny. As it continues to bury itself, and throw the earth behind it, to a great distance, it thus forms itself a winding hole, some six to seven feet deep and thirty feet in length, at the bottom of which it remains in safety. As the fox is not so expert at digging into the earth, it often takes possession of that which has been quitted by the badger, and some say, forces it from its retreat, by laying its excrements at the mouth of the badger's hole.

Oliver Goldsmith
HISTORY OF THE EARTH AND ANIMATED NATURE

Home Sweet Home!

Sir William Beach Thomas 1868-1957

Growing from the ditch below the yews is a tree with a much-divided trunk, springing from a boss not a yard high. This the badgers use for a playing ground, very much as bears will treat a log in a zoo. He jumps in and out between the trunks. The sides of the tree glisten with the rubbing, and the paths this way are trodden hard as a town school's playing yard. You cannot see the signs and not imagine the rough, nightly gambollings of this strange creature so often discussed, so seldom seen.

Few animals, if any, are more faithful to their home. Generation after generation the same earth may be used; and each badger is imbued with an obstinate affection that can scarcely be resisted. Once, many years ago, I saw a badger dug out of his earth, put into a sack, and carried off to a considerable distance before being released. Several of the company stayed by the hole to prevent the animal re-entering. Their joint efforts were wholly vain. Back he came, with lowered head, straight home, brushed past obstructing legs and shouts and blows and disappeared into the outraged earth. Badgers were still living in the same home years later.

The Badger Family

H. Mortimer Batten c.1924

Badgers mate for life, and the dog badger is undoubtedly a father in the true sense. He has been known to save his mate and her cubs by walling them in at the dead end of the hole and selling his own life in their defence. Moreover, I have evidence enough to satisfy myself that if one of the parents be taken from his mate and cubs it will, if its desperate efforts to escape do not succeed, die of sorrow at its loss.

The young, two or three in number, are born in the early spring, and it is generally about April ere they stir far afield with their parents, their first ventures taking the form of delightful root and beetle-hunting expeditions. They are sleepy, placid little beasts, much like little pigs in looks and temperament, and though I have handled quite big cubs recently taken from the earth, I have never known one to try to bite. I have known the little fellows to growl most tremendously, but there was absolutely nothing behind it, as they were glad enough to snuggle down in one's arms, and merely hung like limp puddings when lifted by the skin of the shoulders – still growling in the most terrible manner! One becomes much attached to a tame badger owing to its quiet ways and the manner it looks you straight in the face with its little almond-shaped eyes, and the placid, stolid little cubs cannot fail to win one's heart.

The Life Story
of a Badger

"Gamekeeper"

He was born near the foot of a precipitous headland which a wall shut off from the neighbouring farm. The isolation of the sett had induced his mother to litter there, and when after the birth of her two cubs day succeeded day without any intrusion from an enemy, she all but shook off the misgivings that had at first constantly haunted her as to their safety. So great indeed became her confidence in the security of her surroundings that she even ventured to take the cubs outside the earth that the sun might bathe them with its rays. Whilst they slept she kept watch and ward over them. Occasionally, wearied by her roamings through the dewy morning-grass and lulled by the cries of nesting wildfowl, she would fall into a deep slumber, awaking in a fright at the thought that her cubs might have been stolen from her side, but becoming composed when she saw them still on their couches amongst the seapinks, where they lay blinking at the sunset.

In rainy or chilly weather she kept to the "earth" where, as night approached, the cubs shook off their drowsiness and awaited her summons to go out to play. At the call they followed, frisking at her heels as she led to the one bit of level sward where they could enjoy

their gambols without fear of falling over the cliff. The mother joined in all their games and frequently left herself bare time to reach the foraging ground and get the food she needed, before dawn stole over the uplands and hurried her home. In her absence the cubs remained in the "earth," contentedly enough at first, but with an ever-growing discontent at being left behind. She turned a deaf ear to their plaints, however, until she thought the young creatures fit to accompany her. Then she took them, mad with delight, up the zizgag to the summit of the headland.

Full of wonderment at the strange world to which they were being introduced, the cubs were slow to settle to their lessons, but when they did, they profited so quickly by their mother's instruction that in a few nights they became adept in turning over the stones and muzzling amongst the heather-stems where the insects harboured on which they were chiefly to subsist. The old badger, jealous of their safety, kept listening whilst they foraged, but nothing happened to justify her fears. The only sound that even caused the cubs to prick their ears was the bark of a fox on the hills beyond the homestead.

Before a fortnight had passed every yard of the cliff-top has been ransacked for prey again and again, till, finding it hard to pick up a living, the male cub, ever more forward than his sister, longed to reach the field he could see between the crevices of the piled stones. He knew it was forbidden ground, but that only made it the more tempting; and at last seizing the opportunity when his mother was grubbing in a thick bush, he scrambled over the wall and succeeded in getting half-way across the enclosure before he was discovered and brought back. The incorrigible fellow broke bounds again the next night; whereupon his mother, recognizing that the headland was exhausted as a feeding ground, brushed aside her apprehensions and led him and his sister to the cultivated land where food was abundant.

There they might have roamed and regaled themselves without molestation had they kept to the pastures, but unfortunately, in their extended round, they encroached on a piece of wheat and not only made a wide road across it but, what caused even more damage, rolled in a dozen places on either side of their track. This favourite resort of the badgers occupied a remote corner of the holding and, partly perhaps because of this, remained long unvisited by the farmer. At last, however, the trespass was noticed. At a glance the farmer knew who had wrought the havoc and as quickly formed his plan of retribution against the delinquents. During the dinner hour he said to his son in a voice that showed he was still angry: "They badgers have made a tarble mess of the Five Acres: set a 'grain' in the brambly corner by the Tinners' Field: I see they come in there"; and soon after milking-time the son set a running noose at the mouth of the creep. Three nights later the female cub was caught, and in the morning the farmer found her in the wire dead.

Henceforth the old badger centered all her care and affection on the surviving cub. Abandoning that dangerous beat, she took him in every other direction, and before the summer had passed made him acquainted with every hill and valley for a radius of five miles about the sett. Once they reached a croft six miles away and just as they were about to turn homewards came on what they had for over a week been seeking in vain — a wasps' nest. It was very late, but the temptation to stay and dig it out was too great to resist, and the old badger, conscious that much delay meant lying out, made frantic efforts to secure the prize betimes, so that they might reach the "earth" before sunrise. But the ground proved hard and rocky; and though to kill the wasps that kept stinging her, she rolled but once, she was fully two hours in getting at the combs. The cakes, full of grubs, were worth all the pain and trouble in the opinion of the cub, who, if he had a little part in the labour of excavation, came in for a big share of the feast. He thought as he swallowed the luscious morsels that he had never eaten anything so delicious, not excepting the ripe gooseberries in the farmer's garden, the night his mother overturned the big hive. After gobbling up the last bit of comb, the slow-footed creatures, without stopping to drink in the stream hard by, made for their distant home as fast as their pads could carry them. But the race between them and the sun was hopeless. Many hills stood in their course; and they had scarcely completed half the journey before the dawn, gilding the crags, warned them to seek immediate harbourage. To lie down in the stubble they were crossing was out of the question, so they hurried over the brow and, threading the loose rocks, took to the brake that mantled the slope below. There they curled up under the densest of the furze and tried to compose themselves to rest.

Despite the pain from the stings in her nose, the old badger soon fell asleep; but the cub, though unstung, lay awake listening to the strange, disquieting noises that from time to time rose out of the valley. Now it was the rumbling of a cart, now the cries of the miller's wife scaring the pigs from the garden, and late in the forenoon, when he was about to doze, the braying of a jackass on the lower edge of the brake. This was more than his nerves could stand, and in terror he nestled closer to his mother and wished himself back in the sett. But the worst was over; in the hush that succeeded, nothing could be heard but the drowsy drone of insects and the splashing of the water from the wheel, sounds that both allayed his fears and served him for a slumber-song. He was thinking of wasp-combs when sleep claimed him. The sun had gone down before he arose and followed his mother to the hill-crest beyond the stream, whence rugged downs stretch to a craggy ridge that had the harvest moon above it. The line they took led straight for home, but half-way over the heathery waste they turned aside in search of food, and on reaching the top fell again to foraging, their silvery-grey coats harmonizing with the hoary boulders amongst which they quested. Presently the badger called the cub to her and, descending the abrupt slope, made for the cultivated land and so came to the farm over which they had so often roamed. There was no sound from the homestead as they stole by, and before a cock crowed they were near enough to the cliffs to catch the cries of the seafowl, astir in the grey dawn. Side by side they climbed the boundary-wall and crossed the summit of the headland, but on reaching the dizzy zigzag leading to the sett, the cub dropped behind his mother and remained on the heap after she had disappeared into the "earth". There he stood turning his head quickly from one to other of the two islands whence came the clamour of the fowl, till presently, and after a glance up the cliff, he too passed out of sight.

Both were glad to be abed in the safe den once more, and never again, whilst they remained together, did they sleep in any other lair. It is true that they narrowly escaped lying out on the occasion when they journeyed to a distant valley and feasted on the beechmast with which a gale had strewed the ground. That, however, was a mere accident. Indeed, it was fear of being belated that induced the badger to essay a short cut where she wasted much time before she could extricate herself from the maze of hollows in which she became involved. She was glad to leave the bewildering place behind; but the cub was so pleased with it, and especially with a sort of refuge in the midst of it, that he unhesitatingly bent his steps thither when driven from the sett and forced to seek a home for himself. It was not his mother who expelled him, but the savage old boar she had taken up with, who would not allow the cub to sleep in the "earth" a single day after he was established there.

Late on a black December night he left the headland never to return. The loud chatterings of the tyrant were yet ringing in his ears as he crossed the boundary wall, but the recollection of the delectable spot ahead cheered him, and by the time he was over the ridge he was more troubled about the direction he should follow than by the thought of the brute he was fleeing from. On, on he travelled, and, as luck would have it, straight for his destination, which he reached in the early hours of the morning. He could not mistake it. There was the jagged Cairn, there at its foot was the ring of the sward circling the furze he had twice rounded on that eventful night, and further, there was the stream whose babbling had caught his ears and shortened his quest. He was in no mood for foraging, so, after he had quenched his thirst, he made for a crevice in the Cairn and curled up at the end of the rift it led to. He was very happy to be where he was, and yet he could not shake off the sense of forlorn abandonment that haunted him until fatigue had its way and he fell asleep. He was awake at dusk; but not before the stars showed did he sally out and begin driving a tunnel under the Cairn. He continued to work at this nightly until its length and the den he fashioned at its extremity were to his liking. With this "earth" he was content only for a while, and before March was out he had enlarged it into a sett with three entrances and with galleries and dens on every side.

The heaps of fresh soil he had fetched out caught the eye of a vixen on the look-out for a home, and finding the unoccupied chambers dry and clean she decided to litter in one of them. The badger did not resent the appropriation of a corner of his roomy abode nor complain of the squealing of the whelps when they came, but he did envy the vixen the young rabbits, the goslings, and above all, a fine white cockerel which the dog-fox brought her. It was whilst foraging on the downs that he used to meet Reynard, frequently at first, but less so as time went on, till at last when the cubs were able to accompany the vixen on her rounds he lost sight of the fox altogether. Then he began to be annoyed by the habit vixen and whelps had fallen into of returning late to the sett and disturbing his rest. For several weeks he bit his paw and said nothing, but when, after harvest, bad hours became the rule and not the exception, he resolved to put up with such unnatural ways no longer. The plans of the wild creature, however, like the plans of man, are often upset by something quite unforeseen; and so it was with the badger.

On the very morning he returned to the sett to await the dissolute crew and have it out with them, he found to his dismay that the "earth" had been stopped. At the sight he forgot all about the foxes, and, after vainly trying to scratch a way in, he stole down to the brake, lay up

under a rock in its midst and fell soundly asleep. Before the sun was far above the horizon he was rudely aroused by a pack of fox-hounds who would have worried him to death had it not been that the narrow approach to his refuge made it impossible for more than one hound to reach him at a time. So he was able to keep them at bay and even to inflict more harm than he received. But the rock could not save him from the pandemonium which assailed his sensitive ears; and this he had to endure until his maddened assailants were whipped off by the huntsman. Despite this experience the badger kept to the sett, though afterwards, on finding the holes stopped, he shunned the brake and sought the old harbourage in the recess of the Cairn. Thus he escaped further persecution from the hounds and would have been as happy as the winter nights were long, but for the farm labourers and dogs who ravaged that part of the countryside until they had killed every badger except himself.

All October through, the badger, dreading to be taken by these midnight marauders, never once ventured to roam beyond the edge of the downs, but in November a longing for the companionship of his kind possessed him so strongly that he swept aside his fears and went boldly forth in search of a mate. Day after day he slept out, night after night he resumed his quest, and at last met with a sow of his own age. But his troubles were not yet at an end, for scarcely had he exchanged licks with her before another boar came up on her line and rushed at him like a thing infuriated. The fight that ensued lasted till the sun rose, when his rival was glad to drag himself away from the scene of conflict in order to escape further punishment. The badger was more blown than hurt and, as soon as he recovered his wind, was all for returning to the sett under the Cairn, but the sow would have him come to her own country, and in the end he yielded and followed whither she led.

And what a wild country it seemed, even in his eyes, with its tangled valleys, its rugged slopes and never a patch of cultivated ground. Wonder changed to amazement when he came on the wasteheap of an abandoned mine, a heap to which his excavations were as wormcasts. He was even more struck by the vastness of the sett that was to be the home of himself and his mate. It covered over an acre of ground and was so riddled with holes that the earth-stopper had long given up trying to stop it. So the badgers never saw the light of his lantern, nor indeed any light but that of the moon and stars until summer brought glow-worms to dot the brakes and will-o'-th'-wisp to dance over the bogs. The country, it is true, had one serious defect; food was scarce whilst winter lasted and was never very plentiful at the best of times. At the season of bud-bursting, however, the female tore herself away from the whelps and showed her mate the woodland in the low country where wild hyacinths abounded. There they feasted on the delicious bulbs that were to be had for a few scratches of their powerful claws, and thither later they led the cubs, whose delight it was to wander amongst the trees and, following their parents' example, to stretch themselves against the bole of an oak. The woodman saw the marks of their claws, the pits they dug and the prints both big and small where the stream crosses the ride, but he laid no trap and set no snare.

In that wood and over the wild waste about the sett the badger wanders today. Fear no longer shadows his steps and it is likely that he will live to the full span of years, that his last trail will lead to the cave, unknown to man, where for ages his kind have crept to die.

THE GREAT DIGGER

Using its strong forepaws, the badger excavates lengthy tunnels, branching off in several directions. The sett is sometimes shared by a fox, or a family of rabbits whose presence is tolerated.

BABY BADGERS

Badger babies (usually two or three in a litter) are endearing and very playful. They will romp and chase and tumble for hours outside the sett.

NOCTURNAL HABITS

Badgers emerge from their setts only at night, and are extremely shy and elusive.

BADGER BRAVERY

The badger's courage under attack is legendary, especially if its young are threatened. This may be why it was the victim of the cruel sport of baiting by dogs.

Badger Tracks

RUBBING POSTS

In order to keep his coat groomed and clean, the badger uses the trees around his sett as rubbing posts.

TAME BADGERS

If caught young, badgers can be tamed. They have been known to settle down with the family dog, and enjoy basking in front of a good fire!

BADGER HYGIENE

Badger setts are notably clean, and have special sections in which they store left-over food. They are careful to remove any rotting food or dirt from the living quarters, and change setts regularly. During winter, the badger stays inside the sett, and walls up the entrance to keep cosy and warm inside.

The Botanist

*B*ut even though flowers may truly be said to grow everywhere, yet a knowledge of their favourite habitats will prove extremely useful at times when we are searching for certain desired species. Some prefer the darkest woods; while others are only to be found in spots exposed to the full sun; and meadows, cornfields, shady banks, ditches, ponds, streams, and the sea-shore, all bring forth their own peculiar flowers.

Your collecting apparatus will be much the same as that used for collecting Ferns, viz.; a rather large vasculum, a trowel, a knife, and a note-book. A few small boxes will also be useful to contain specimens of small and delicate plants, as well as such ripe fruits as you may meet with.

W. Furneaux:
THE OUTDOOR WORLD

Living Botany

Canon Vaughan c. 1908

There is a strange fascination in the search after rare plants, especially in localities rendered interesting by the "record" of some early observer. The purely scientific student may carry on his investigations in the laboratory, the field-botanist seeks the open air. With Izaac Walton he sallies forth into the meadows "chequered with water-lilies and lady-smocks," or along the "high honey-suckle hedge," or "under the willow-trees by the water-side." With John Ray at Black Notley he knows the "habitat" of every rare plant in the parish, or like Gilbert White he visits season by season every choice species in the neighbourhood – the mezereon among the brushwood at the top of the Hanger, the herb-paris in the Church Litten Coppice, or the marsh cinquefoil in the bogs of Bin's-pond.

In this way only is it possible to become acquainted with the growth and habit of species. A dried specimen in the herbarium is not the same thing as the living plant in its own surroundings. *Scilla verna*, be it never so carefully pressed, is but a sorry likeness of the exquisitely beautiful Vernal Squill as it may be seen in thousands on the short sandy turf above the magnificent cliffs of Cornwall and South Wales. It is difficult to recognize in the dark, mummified specimen labelled, "*Ophrys apifera, Huds,*" the splendid Bee-orchis of our Hampshire downs. Hence many teachers of botany have given instruction out of doors as well as in the lecture-room.

The Pursuit of Botany

Gilbert White 1720-1795

The standing objection to botany has always been, that it is a pursuit that amuses the fancy and exercises the memory, without improving the mind or advancing any real knowledge; and where the science is carried no farther than a mere systematic classification, the charge is but too true. But the botanist that is desirous of wiping off this aspersion should be by no means content with a list of names; he should study plants philosophically, should investigate the laws of vegetation, should examine the powers and virtues of efficacious herbs, should promote their cultivation, and graft the gardener, the planter, and the husbandman, on the phytologist. Not that system is by any means to be thrown aside; without system the field of nature would be a pathless wilderness: but system should be subservient to, not the main object of, pursuit.

Vegetation is highly worthy of our attention; and in itself is of the upmost consequence to mankind, and productive of many of the greatest comforts and elegancies of life. To plants we owe timber, bread, beer, honey, wine, oil, linen, cotton, etc., what not only strengthens our hearts, and exhilarates our spirits, but what secures from inclemencies of weather and adorns our persons. Man, in his true state of nature, seems to

be subsisted by spontaneous vegetation: in middle climes, where grasses prevail, he mixes some animal food with the produce of the field and garden: and it is towards the polar extremes only that, like his kindred bears and wolves, he gorges himself with flesh alone, and is driven, to what hunger has never been known to compel the very beasts to prey on his own species.

THE CHALK CRESCENT

The Downs have always fascinated botanists. They are a crescent of gentle chalk hills, ranging from the tip of Flamborough head in the North, to the fringes of Devon in the South.

DOWNLAND FLOWERS

The more common flowers of the Downs include white and yellow bedstraw, the clustered bellflower, bird's foot trefoil (left), ladies' fingers, and the quaintly named squinancy-wort of the old herbalists. The botanist also finds wild anenome, pasque flowers, and viper's bugloss here.

SHEEP GRAZING

The surface of the Downs has been kept closely grazed by flocks of sheep for hundreds of years, and this has created a particular habitat for the botanist to explore.

Botanist's Rambles

BUTTERFLIES

Part of the pleasure of a botanical ramble on the Downs is the infinite joy of walking amongst butterflies. The Large Blue, which fed upon wild thyme, is now sadly extinct.

DOWNLAND TREES

As well as the juniper which grows in profusion on the Downs, there are yews, beeches and guelder-roses (right).

BRITISH FLORA

After the death of Gerarde, the famous herbalist, Thomas Johnson published the first local catalogue of British plants. Then, in 1690, John Ray (above) published the earliest systematic flora of our native plants.

OLIVER GOLDSMITH
1730-1774. Dr Johnson's epitaph to the much-loved author of THE VICAR OF WAKEFIELD, and THE DESERTED VILLAGE said "He adorned whatever he touched". Our extract is from his fascinating work, HISTORY OF THE EARTH AND ANIMATED NATURE (1774).

GERARD MANLEY HOPKINS
1844-1889 (below). Priest and poet, he introduced highly original 'modern' techniques into Victorian verse. His intense love of nature is expressed in such classics as PIED BEAUTY.

W. H. HUDSON
1841-1922. Born in South America, he is best-known for his exquisite writing on birds, but also wrote on more general natural history subjects. His subjects include the bird life of Argentina and Britain.

JOHN MASEFIELD
1878-1967. By the age of 17, he had been in the merchant navy, deserted ship and become a vagrant and a poet. His idyllic early childhood and his years at sea form a dual inspiration for his work. Among his most famous seafaring poems are *'I must go down to the sea again'*. He was made poet laureate in 1930.

$\mathcal{T}he$ $\mathcal{W}riters$

WILLIAM SHAKESPEARE
1564-1616. Poet and playwright, he is widely considered the greatest writer in the English language. A Warwickshire man born and bred, he loved nature as much as the theatre, and his songs and poems draw on and form part of the English folk tradition. Our extract is from his magical A MIDSUMMER NIGHT'S DREAM.

EDWARD THOMAS
1878-1917. A sensitive and perceptive observer of nature, he found his voice as a poet only a few years before he died in the First World War. Always true to what he saw and felt, he won the respect of fellow-poets before winning a wider posthumous fame.

GILBERT WHITE
1720-1793 (left). An amateur naturalist, whose love of and gift for describing nature resulted in the classic NATURAL HISTORY AND ANTIQUITIES OF SELBORNE (in Hampshire where he lived most of his life). One of his companions was a tame bat.

Acknowledgements

PAGES 4/5
On the South Downs by Robert Angelo Kidderminster (1849-c.1923), Fine Art Photographic Library.

PAGE 7
Herbs/Thyme, Mary Evans Picture Library.

PAGE 9
There Sleeps Titania by John Simmons (active 1882-1889), The Bridgeman Art Library.

PAGE 11
Saint-Foin in Bloom by John Samuel Raven (1829-1877), Fine Art Photographic Library.

PAGE 13
Fairy and Sprites in the Undergrowth by Georges Picard (born 1857), Galerie George, London. The Bridgeman Art Library.

PAGES 14/15
From the Chronicle of England Vol.11, King Edward III at a joust held in honour of the Countess of Salisbury, School of Loyset Liedet, late 15th century. The Bridgeman Art Library.
A Perfect Day by James Thomas Linell (1820-1905), Fine Art Photographic Library.
Thymus Chamaedrys (Larger Wild Thyme), The Mansell Collection.
Insects/Bees, Mary Evans Picture Library.
Toilet/Bathing 1914 by Fred Pegram from "London's Social Calender", Mary Evans Picture Library.

PAGE 17
The New Book of Trees by Marcus Woodward.

PAGE 19
Poole Harbour from the Isle of Purbeck by Donald Maxwell.

PAGE 21
The South Downs 1886 by Arthur Gilbert (1819-1895), Fine Art Photographic Library.

PAGES 22/23
The Yew Walk, Barncluith, Strathclyde by Ernest Arthur Rowe (active 1885, died 1922), John Spink, Fine Water Colours, London, The Bridgeman Art Library.
Iron Age Funeral, Mary Evans Picture Library.
Katie's Letter by Haynes King (1831-1904), Atkinson Gallery, Southport, Lancashire. The Bridgeman Art Library.
A London Gin Shop by R & G Cruikshank (1820) from Prince Egan's life in London, Mary Evans Picture Library.

PAGE 28/29
Dinner at Haddo House by A.E.Emslie (1884), National Portrait Gallery.

PAGE 33
Kestrels (the male in the foreground) by A.W.Seaby.

PAGES 34/35
A Little Luncheon at Timmins by Du Maurier in Punch, Mary Evans Picture Library.
Kestrel by Morris, Mary Evans Picture Library.
Equipment for Falconry by M. Wold (1853), by courtesy of the Victoria & Albert Museum, London, The Bridgeman Art Library.
The Falconer by Benno Friedrich Toermer (19th century), Christie's, London, The Bridgeman Art Library.

PAGE 37
Badger, The Mansell Collection.

PAGES 52/53
Badger by Francis Barlow (1626-1702), Roy Miles Fine Painting, London, The Bridgeman Art Library.
Dogs Baiting a Badger (c.1870), Stern (Art Dealers) Co., London, The Bridgeman Art Library.
Sheep resting on a woodland track (1870) by Frederick William Hume (1816-1884), Fine Art Photographic Library.

PAGE 55
Botanists at Work (1802) Frontispiece to Curtis, Florra Londonionis, Mary Evans Picture Library.

PAGE 57
Portrait of the Botanist Anne Pratt with an open Fern Specimen Book on her lap, Anon., English School, Fine Art Photographic Library.

PAGES 60/61
Sussex Downs by Thomas Collier R.I. (1840-1891), Victoria & Albert Museum, London, The Bridgeman Art Library.
The Sheep Pool by Edward Stott (1859-1918), Fine Art Photographic Library.
Butterflies by Charles Sims R.A., R.W.S. (1837-1928), Fine Art Photographic Library.
Downs, The Bridgeman Art Library.
John Ray, The Mansell Collection.
The Large Blue Butterfly, The Mansell Collection.

PAGES 62/63
Gerard Manley Hopkins, National Portrait Gallery.
John Masefield, William Shakespeare and Gilbert White, Mary Evans Picture Library.